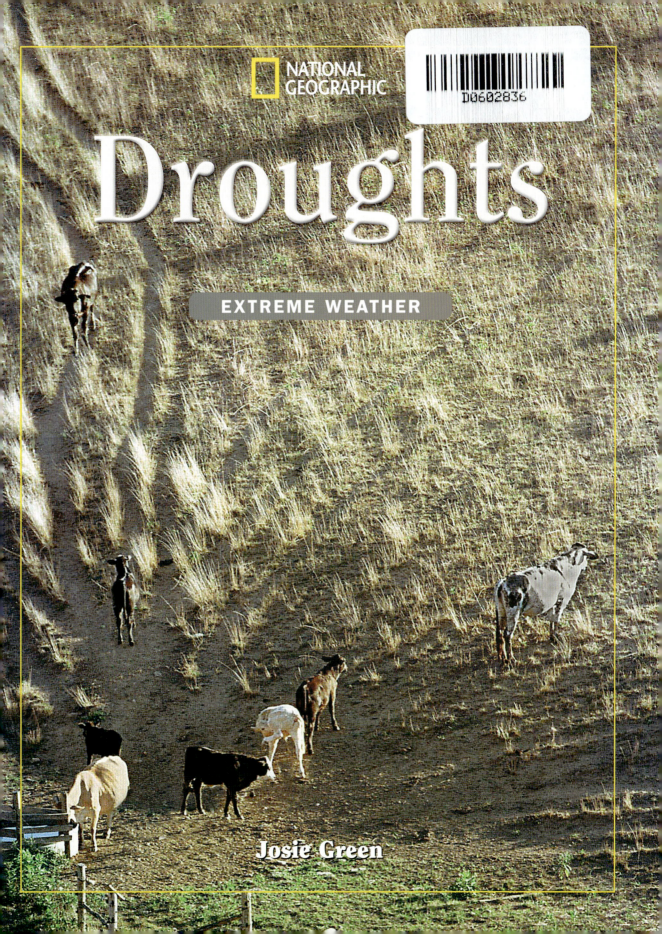

NATIONAL GEOGRAPHIC

Droughts

EXTREME WEATHER

Josie Green

PICTURE CREDITS
Cover: © James A. Sugar/Corbis

page 1 © Williams Michael/Corbis Sygma; page 4 (bottom left) Despotovic Dusko/Corbis Sygma; page 5 (top) © AFP/Corbis; page 6 © Raymond Gehman/Corbis; page 7 (top) © Adrian Arbib/Corbis; page 9 (left) © Bruce Miller/Corbis; page 9 (right) © Matt Brown/Corbis; page 10 © Jim Richardson/Corbis; page 11 © William James Warren/Corbis; page 12 © Richard Glover; Ecoscene/Corbis; page 13 (bottom) Stock Image Group/SPL; page 15 Stock Image Group/SPL; page 23 © Coo-ee Picture Library; page 24 Courtesy of Commonwealth Bureau of Meteorology/Katsuhiro Abe; page 26 © Penny Tweedie/Corbis.

Produced through the worldwide resources of the National Geographic Society, John M. Fahey, Jr., President and Chief Executive Officer; Gilbert M. Grosvenor, Chairman of the Board; Nina D. Hoffman, Executive Vice President and President, Books and Education Publishing Group.

PREPARED BY NATIONAL GEOGRAPHIC SCHOOL PUBLISHING
Ericka Markman, Senior Vice President and President, Children's Books and Education Publishing Group; Steve Mico, Vice President and Editorial Director; Marianne Hiland, Executive Editor; Richard Easby, Editorial Manager; Jim Hiscott, Design Manager; Kristin Hanneman, Illustrations Manager; Matt Wascavage, Manager of Publishing Services; Sean Philpotts, Production Manager.

EDITORIAL MANAGEMENT
Morrison BookWorks, LLC

PROGRAM CONSULTANTS
Dr. Shirley V. Dickson, Program Director, Literacy, Education Commission of the States; James A. Shymansky, E. Desmond Lee Professor of Science Education, University of Missouri-St. Louis.

National Geographic Theme Sets program developed by Macmillan Education Australia, Pty Limited.

Published by the National Geographic Society
1145 17th Street, N.W.
Washington, D.C. 20036-4688

ISBN: 978-0-7922-4722-7
ISBN: 0-7922-4722-1

Product 41962

Printed in China

13 14 15 16 17 18 19 20 21
10 9 8 7 6 5

Contents

💡 Extreme Weather. 4

Weather and Drought. 6

💡 Think About the Key Concepts. 17

Visual Literacy
Weather Maps. 18

Genre Study
Explanations. 20

The Great Australian Drought, 1982–1983. 21

💡 Apply the Key Concepts. .27

Research and Write
Create Your Own Explanation. 28

Glossary. 31

Index. 32

Extreme Weather

The weather affects people's lives in many different ways. Weather helps people decide what clothes to wear, or what to do in their spare time. However, the weather can also be a matter of life and death. Extreme weather can be very severe. Droughts, floods, tornadoes, and hurricanes are all examples of extreme weather.

💡 Key Concepts ....

1. Conditions in the atmosphere, such as air pressure, create weather.
2. Clouds give meteorologists clues about what is happening in the atmosphere.
3. Tools and technology help meteorologists gather data about weather.

Four Kinds of Extreme Weather

Droughts

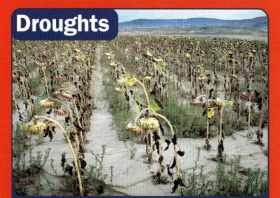

Droughts happen when there is a lack of rain.

Floods

Floods happen when too much water flows over the land.

In this book you will learn about the causes and effects of droughts like this one.

Tornadoes

Tornadoes are spinning wind funnels that create strong suction.

Hurricanes

Hurricanes are powerful storms with strong winds and heavy rains.

Weather and Drought

You may not like the weather when it rains. But imagine if it didn't rain. There would be no water. Think about how difficult your life would be without water. **Droughts** occur when it doesn't rain for a long time in a place that normally gets some rain. Droughts can badly affect people and the land.

A Dry Time

When there is a drought, the land becomes very dry. Rivers, lakes, and soil can dry up. Crops can die. Animals can die from lack of water or food. Trees become so dry that forest fires can start easily. Forest fires can kill animals and destroy people's homes.

Forest fires can start easily during a drought.

Long droughts can cause **famine**. Famine occurs when people do not have enough to eat or drink. Many people can die when there is a famine.

Droughts can occur all over the world. Look at the map. You will see the places where droughts can occur.

Grain is given to people during a famine in Kenya.

Places Where Droughts Can Occur

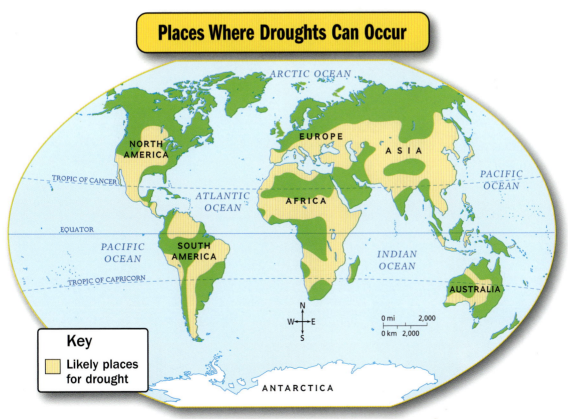

ARCTIC OCEAN

NORTH AMERICA

EUROPE

ASIA

PACIFIC OCEAN

TROPIC OF CANCER

ATLANTIC OCEAN

AFRICA

EQUATOR

PACIFIC OCEAN

SOUTH AMERICA

INDIAN OCEAN

TROPIC OF CAPRICORN

AUSTRALIA

N
W   E
S

0 mi   2,000
0 km   2,000

Key
Likely places for drought

ANTARCTICA

Key Concept 1 **Conditions in the atmosphere, such as air pressure, create weather.**

Where Rain Comes From

To understand what causes droughts, you first have to understand where rain comes from. Rain comes from water in oceans, rivers, and lakes. The sun warms the water. This changes some of the water into water **vapor**. Vapor is very small drops of water in the air. This vapor rises into the **atmosphere**. The atmosphere is the layer of air that surrounds Earth.

As the vapor rises higher, it cools down. As it cools, the vapor turns into bigger drops of water. These drops form clouds. As the air gets colder, the drops get bigger and heavier. Then, they fall back to Earth as rain.

> **atmosphere**
> the layer of air that surrounds Earth

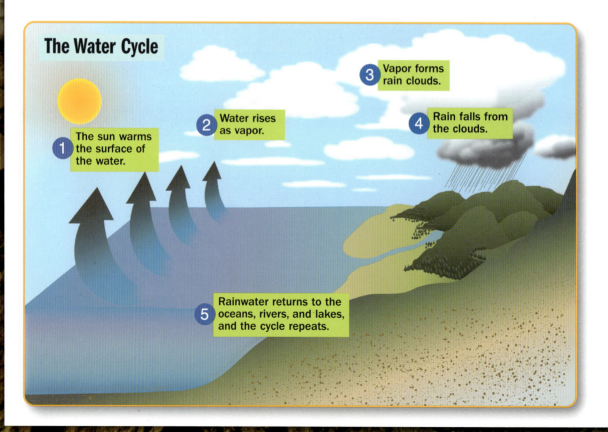

The Water Cycle

1 The sun warms the surface of the water.

2 Water rises as vapor.

3 Vapor forms rain clouds.

4 Rain falls from the clouds.

5 Rainwater returns to the oceans, rivers, and lakes, and the cycle repeats.

Air Pressure

The air above Earth is always pressing down on Earth's surface. This is called **air pressure**. Air pressure is not always the same.

Warm air is lighter, so it tends to rise. Then, there is less air pressing down on Earth. This is called **low air pressure**. The rising air carries water vapor into the sky. The water vapor turns into clouds. Low air pressure often leads to rain.

When air above Earth cools, it becomes heavy and sinks. Sinking air forms **high air pressure**. The heavy air can stop water vapor from rising and forming rain clouds. So, high air pressure often leads to dry weather.

When the weather is wet, the air pressure is usually low.

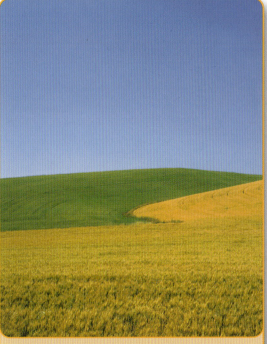

When the weather is clear, the air pressure is usually high.

Why Droughts Occur

Droughts can occur for many different reasons. The most common reason is high air pressure that lasts for a long time.

This farmer's field is very dry due to a drought.

High Air Pressure

When there is high air pressure in an area, it usually does not rain. High air pressure usually does not last long. After a while, warm air rises and rain clouds form. But sometimes, the air does not rise. The air pressure stays high for a long time, so rain clouds do not form.

Droughts with Rain Clouds

Sometimes, rain clouds form in places where there are often droughts, but it still does not rain. This happens when it is hot and dry. The hot, dry air heats the drops of rain as they fall toward Earth. The heat turns the raindrops back into vapor before they reach the ground.

There may be clouds during a drought, but that does not always mean that it will rain.

Looking at Clouds

meteorologists
scientists who study the weather

Meteorologists are people who study the weather. One way meteorologists can **predict** the weather is by looking at clouds. There are many types of clouds. Some clouds help meteorologists understand what weather conditions have caused a drought. Some types of clouds may show that a drought is going to end.

Cirrus Clouds

Cirrus clouds are very high in the sky. Cirrus clouds are thin and wispy. It is very cold in the sky where cirrus clouds form so they are made of ice, not drops of water. Cirrus clouds do not bring rain that can end a drought.

Thin, wispy cirrus clouds do not bring rain.

Cumulus Clouds

Cumulus clouds are puffy clouds. Cumulus clouds can be a good sign during a drought. If cumulus clouds grow, they can bring rain. But big cumulus clouds are not always good news during a drought.

Sometimes, big cumulus clouds do not bring rain. Any rain falling from these clouds is heated by warm air and becomes vapor before it reaches the ground.

Small cumulus clouds can grow into big storm clouds.

Nimbostratus Clouds

Nimbostratus clouds can show that a drought will end. These clouds look like a thick blanket of cloud. They bring steady rain, often for days on end. This is the best type of rain to end a drought.

Nimbostratus are thick clouds that block out the sun.

Predicting Drought

Meteorologists have ways of predicting drought. They use tools to gather **data**, or information. Computers turn the data into weather maps. Meteorologists use the weather maps to see if a drought may occur. Meteorologists can also predict if rain may come to end a drought. Thermometers, hygrometers, and weather satellites are some of the tools that meteorologists use.

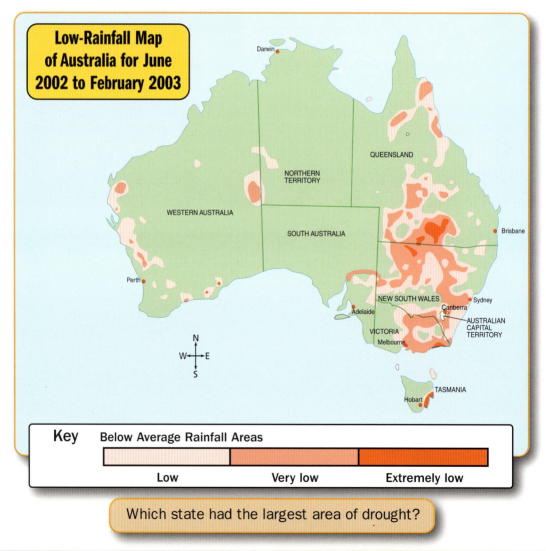

Low-Rainfall Map of Australia for June 2002 to February 2003

Key — Below Average Rainfall Areas: Low, Very low, Extremely low

Which state had the largest area of drought?

Thermometers

Thermometers show how hot or cold the air is. During a drought, the air temperature can be very hot. Droughts most often occur at the hottest time of the year. If the air temperature is very hot for a long time, meteorologists can predict that a drought will continue.

Meteorologists keep thermometers inside a Stephenson screen. This is a box made of wooden slats. The box keeps out direct sunlight, but lets air flow through. This way, the thermometer can record the temperature of the air and not the temperature of the sunlight.

A meteorologist reads a thermometer inside a Stephenson screen.

Hygrometers

Hygrometers measure **humidity**. Humidity is the amount of moisture in the air. Humidity is low when there is a drought because the air is very dry. If there is low humidity for a long time, meteorologists can predict that a drought will continue.

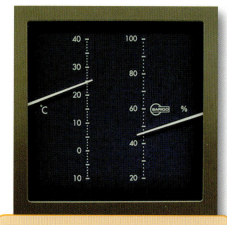

The measurements on the right of this hygrometer show humidity.

Weather Satellites

Weather **satellites** travel around Earth. They take photos of clouds. They send the photos to weather offices. Meteorologists can tell from the photos which kinds of clouds are forming. They can then predict if rain is likely to occur and end a drought.

A weather satellite in space

Think about what you read. Think about the pictures and diagrams. Use these to answer the questions. Share what you think with others.

1. Name one kind of extreme weather. What conditions lead to this weather?

2. What can meteorologists learn about the weather from studying clouds?

3. What tools do meteorologists use to forecast the weather?

4. How does extreme weather affect people and the land?

Weather Maps

Weather maps contain information that helps you understand the weather.

Look back at the weather map on page 14. It is a weather map of Australia. The map shows which places had low rainfall for a certain period.

The weather map on page 19 is a different kind of weather map. It shows conditions that might cause dry weather in the southern United States. To read a weather map, follow the steps below.

How to Read a Weather Map

1. **Read the title to learn what the map shows.**
   What is this weather map about?

2. **Read the key to learn what the symbols stand for.**
   What do the lines show? What do the letters L and H stand for?

3. **Study the information on the map.**
   Which state is likely to be having a drought? Why do you think that?

4. **Think about what you have learned.**
   If it was likely to rain soon in a city, would you expect to see a letter H or a letter L near that city on the map?

Drought Conditions in the United States

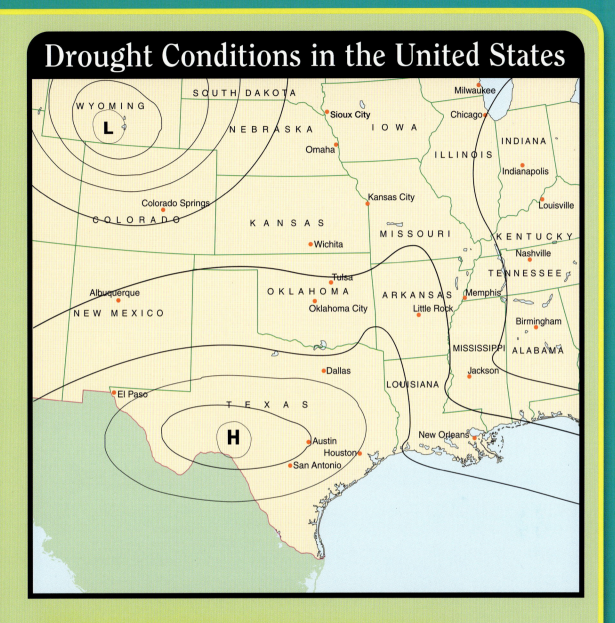

Key

L   Area of low air pressure

H   Area of high air pressure

⟋   Isobars – join areas that have the same air pressure

Explanations

An **explanation** can tell how and why something happened. The article starting on page 21 tells about one specific weather event. It explains what happened, why it happened, and what effects it had on the people and land.

An explanation includes the following:

The Introduction
The introduction gives the reader an overview, or the big picture of what the explanation is about.

Body Paragraphs
The body paragraphs make up most of the writing in the explanation. They provide the information and details that help to explain the event.

The Conclusion
The conclusion summarizes or ties together the information in the explanation.

The Great Australian Drought, 1982-1983

Droughts occur when it doesn't rain for a long time in a place that usually gets rain. Australia had a very bad drought in 1982 and 1983. It was the worst drought in Australia for over 100 years.

New South Wales, Victoria, South Australia, and Tasmania were the driest states. They were hit hardest by the drought. Animals died and crops failed. The drought affected thousands of people.

The **title** tells you the topic.

The **introduction** tells you what the explanation will be about.

Maps, diagrams, charts, and photographs help you picture what you are reading.

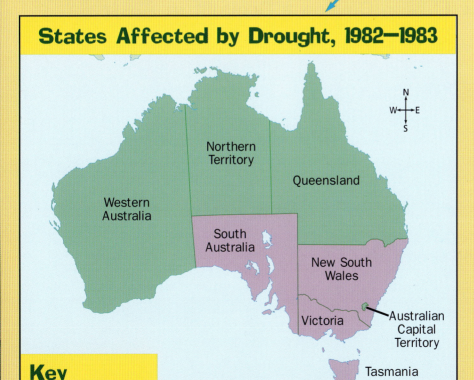

States Affected by Drought, 1982–1983

Northern Territory

Queensland

Western Australia

South Australia

New South Wales

Victoria

Australian Capital Territory

Tasmania

N
W E
S

Key

Affected states

The Cause of the Drought

Body paragraphs give details.

Scientists think that a weather pattern called El Niño caused the drought in Australia. El Niño causes different weather in different parts of the world. It causes a lot of rain and floods in some places. It causes droughts in other places. El Niño lasts about a year.

In normal weather conditions, warm winds from South America blow from east to west across the Pacific Ocean. The winds carry storms to Australia. These storms bring rain to Australia.

During an El Niño weather pattern, the winds change direction. They blow from west to east across the Pacific Ocean. The storms no longer move across Australia. So Australia gets very little rain during El Niño.

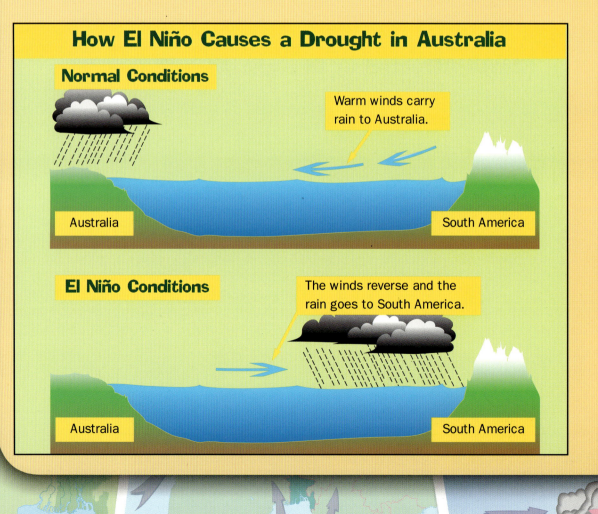

How El Niño Causes a Drought in Australia

Normal Conditions

Warm winds carry rain to Australia.

Australia

South America

El Niño Conditions

The winds reverse and the rain goes to South America.

Australia

South America

How the Drought Began

The drought began in January 1982. El Niño often occurs at this time of year. But this year, El Niño was stronger than usual.

By April 1982, there was very little rainfall in eastern Australia. In June and July there were short, sharp frosts. The skies were clear. There were no clouds, and there was still no rain.

September, October, and November were also very dry months in most of eastern Australia. By now there was very little water available. Many towns ran out of water.

There was also very little water in the rivers. There was so little water in the Murrumbidgee River that it did not flow at all in some places. It became a row of waterholes.

By December 1982, Australia had recorded one of its lowest ever rainfalls for the time between April and December.

In 1983, this creek in the state of Victoria had nearly dried up.

The Worst of the Drought

The drought was at its worst in February 1983. At this time, the weather was very hot. The temperature was 40–50° Celsius (104–122° Fahrenheit). The forests and fields were very dry. There was record-low rainfall in Tasmania. There was almost no rain at all in Victoria.

Cotton growers were not able to plant their cotton. Wheat farmers could not grow wheat. Sheep and cattle farmers had no grass for their animals to eat, so many animals died.

Then, a very strong wind started to blow from the north. The wind caused severe dust storms.

A dust storm fills the sky in Melbourne, Victoria, during the drought.

Because the forests were dry, forest fires started easily. The fires were quickly spread by the wind. Some of the fires burned for a month.

Many forests were destroyed. More than 2,000 people lost their houses in the fires, and 75 people died.

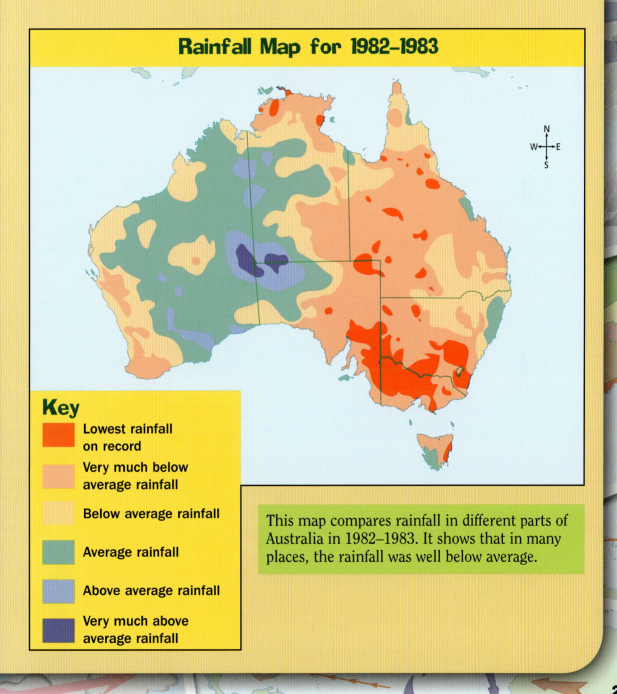

Rainfall Map for 1982–1983

Key

- Lowest rainfall on record
- Very much below average rainfall
- Below average rainfall
- Average rainfall
- Above average rainfall
- Very much above average rainfall

This map compares rainfall in different parts of Australia in 1982–1983. It shows that in many places, the rainfall was well below average.

The Australian drought meant that there was very little grass to feed sheep.

How the Drought Ended

The **conclusion** summarizes the text.

In March 1983, the drought began to break. A large area of low pressure developed over Western Australia. It moved east and brought strong winds with it. Then, the temperature dropped. Finally, heavy rain brought relief from the drought.

The Australian drought of 1982–1983 lasted for more than a year. It affected thousands of people and animals. The drought cost the country more than 3 billion dollars. It was a reminder to Australians of how the weather could change their lives.

Apply the **Key Concepts**

Key Concept 1 Conditions in the atmosphere, such as air pressure, create weather.

Activity

Make a list of weather conditions that can lead to a drought. Then, go to the library and get a book on droughts. Look through the book to find sections about drought weather conditions. Read these sections. Add any new weather conditions you find to your list.

Weather Conditions
1. high air pressure
2.
3.

Key Concept 2 Clouds give meteorologists clues about what is happening in the atmosphere.

Activity

Draw a chart with two columns. In the first column, draw pictures of different kinds of clouds. In the second column, name each kind of cloud and tell what it looks like. Label your chart "Clouds and What They Look Like."

Cloud	Name

Key Concept 3 Tools and technology help meteorologists gather data about weather.

Activity

Research some more information about hygrometers. Find out when hygrometers were invented and how they work. Then write an account of your findings.

Hygrometers
_____
_____
_____

Create Your Own Explanation

There are lots of examples of extreme weather around the world. Some extreme weather may even happen close to where you live. Can you remember a flood or a drought? Can you remember a big storm that turned into a hurricane or caused a tornado?

1. Study the Model

Look back at the description of explanations on page 20. Then, read the article on pages 21–26 again. Look for the examples in the text that tell you this is an explanation. Can you find the opening statement? Can you find the concluding statement? Which paragraphs explain the causes of the weather disaster? Which paragraphs explain the effects of the weather disaster? Look at the diagrams or maps again. Think about how they helped you understand the topic.

2. Choose Your Topic

Now choose one example of an extreme weather event that you would like to find out more about. You may have to start by looking at books on extreme weather, reading newspaper accounts, or using the Internet. Once you've chosen your topic, you're ready to start.

3. Research Your Topic

Ask yourself what you already know about this topic. Do you know enough to write an explanation of how or why it occurred? Probably not. So, you need to make a list of questions that you need to answer. Remember that you are going to write an explanation, so many of your questions may start with "how" or "why." Now go to the library or to the Internet to get your facts.

Monsoon

1. What caused the monsoon?

2. How did the monsoon affect people?

4. Take Notes

Take notes of what you find out. As you find out a new fact, you may find that it leads to another question. Write the new questions down so that you don't forget them. As you write your notes, make a note of the things that you can explain using a diagram or map.

5. Write a Draft

Look back at the facts you found. Do they explain how or why your event occurred? If they do, start writing your draft. You may need to check back with page 20 to remind yourself of the features of an explanation.

6. Revise and Edit

Reread your draft. Does it explain your extreme weather event? Does it have all the features of an explanation? Have you spelled special weather words correctly? Have you drawn charts and maps to help with the explanation?

Present Your Explanation

Now you can share your work. With a group of students, present your explanations as part of a television special report on extreme weather. The program will be called *Explaining Extreme Weather.*

How to Present Your Work

1. **Choose a person in your group to be the anchorperson.**
   That person will introduce each member of the group. The anchorperson will also read the opening statement from each explanation.

2. **Collect the equipment you will need.**
   Before you make your presentation, you will need to transfer your charts and maps to overhead transparencies or to a piece of poster board.

3. **Rehearse your reading.**
   Before you read your explanation you will need to rehearse reading it aloud. Read it aloud several times. Practice looking up at your audience while you are speaking.

4. **When you have finished, be prepared to answer questions.**
   Your audience may ask you to explain something in more detail or review some of the facts.

5. **When you have all made your oral presentations, bind the explanations together and make them into a book.**
   As a group, make a cover for the book. Then, bind all the pages together with staples or yarn.

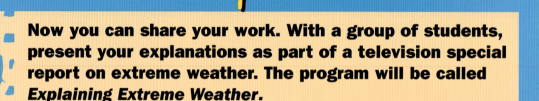

Hailstorms

Hailstorms can cause damage all over the world.

Worst Hailstorms

Some of the worst hailstorms have occurred at these places.

Glossary

air pressure – the effect of air pressing down on Earth's surface

atmosphere – the layer of air that surrounds Earth

data – information that is collected

droughts – long-term lack of rain

famine – a shortage of food or drinking water

high air pressure – a weather condition that occurs when there is a lot of air pressing down on Earth

humidity – the amount of moisture in the air

low air pressure – a weather condition that occurs when there is not much air pressing down on Earth

meteorologists – scientists who study the weather

predict – to guess what might happen in the future

satellites – objects that travel around Earth in space and send information back to Earth

vapor – small drops of water in the air that rise into the atmosphere

Index

air pressure 9–10

atmosphere 8

clouds 8–13, 16

crops 6

drought 4–8, 10–16

famine 7

forest fires 6

meteorologist 12, 14–16

rain 4–6, 8–14, 16

temperature 15

water 4, 6, 8–9, 12

weather 4, 6, 9, 12

weather offices 16